LOOKING FOR THE FACES OF GOD

Front cover handmade paper sculpture "Generations" by Bruria, Santa Monica, California. Photographed by Doug Parker.

Back cover photograph by Hella Hamid.

Book design by Lawrence Watson.

A portion of the proceeds from the sale of this book will be donated to the Buddhist Peace Fellowship.

LOOKING FOR THE FACES OF GOD

DEENA METZGER

PARALLAX PRESS • BERKELEY • CALIFORNIA

OTHER BOOKS BY DEENA METZGER

Skin:Shadows/Silence
Dark Milk
Axis Mundi Poems
The Woman Who Slept With Men to Take the War Out of Them
Tree
What Dinah Thought

PLAYS

The Book of Hags
Milk Fever
Not As Sleepwalkers
Dreams Against the State

FORTHCOMING

Writing For Your Life: Creativity, Imagination and Healing (nonfiction)
A Sabbath Among the Ruins (poetry)

Copyright © 1989, by Deena Metzger, all rights reserved.
Printed in the United States of America.
Second printing, October 1991

Cataloging-in-Publication Data

Metzger, Deena.
   Looking for the faces of God / Deena Metzger. Parallax Press, c1989.
ISBN: 0938077236 : $8.00

89-23139

Thanks to the editors of the following anthologies and
publications in which some of these poems initially appeared:

*The Anthology of Los Angeles Poets, Canticles of Light [recording],
Elmwood Institute Newsletter, Erotic by Nature, Jacaranda Review,
Persona, Pleasures, Redstart Eight Plus, Shirim, Southern California
Poetry, The Listening Life, Invocation L.A., Creation, In My Two Hands*

CONTENTS

MALKUT

TEPHERET

KETHER

This book is dedicated to my companion,
Timber Wolf,
who has always been the door.

MALKUT

ICON

This wooden icon
is the face
of god,
a knife
in a human hand
found it.
I am waiting
for it to speak.
If
there is a sign,
it is

howl of wolf

wet muzzle

gleaming teeth.

BETWEEN THE WORLDS

Flesh like metal,
spirit like mist,

teach me the gait
of the luminous wolves
drinking
from the dark river.

In those waters
the stones sing,
can the world
mend
in this body?

SETTING OUT

Your birth sign:
'Receptive.'
You are always
opening doors.

This drum,
a slit trunk,
once called
through all the trees,
sounds never heard
in a house.
Hunters and gatherers knew
all the animal languages,

now even the whisper
of corn
fades
in the opposing wind.

WHAT SHAKES ME

After breath and light,
everything given to us
from below,
even fire
falling again
out of the sky,
into her dark body.
Nothing is built
until stone
is quarried
or her great arms felled,
cities ground
from her pressed bones.

In Peruvian mines,
each vein
named for
a great whore.

Before the quake,
heaven aglow
from pressed quartz.

My sign is Earth.
The Magi says,
"Live in rubble for a year."
Where am I going
before I return
to myself?

HAGAR SPEAKS

What God sucks into himself,
we must pluck out
and break into pieces.
The wind wears
the face of each tree
and the owl,
this body,
hooting for its portion.

ALCHEMY

This clay
I call my life
has a mouth.
To it,
I put my mouth
begging it to breathe.
Outside the circle,
the gods howl
their own pain without hands.
These shadows
want a body,
need to walk on feet,
to wake up in the rumple of sheets
about their shapes.

I have traveled the longing
of wishing to be with what dies
and I must walk
two stairs of vision into myself
beginning here,
in this density,
this heaviness of earth and water.

> For centuries
> men also worked
> intractable heavy lead
> but then,
> the golem,
> pounded from his own darkness,
> lumbered forth.

Now, from the blind outside
of language
we are called to the task again,
to bring breath
to these mouths
which do not know
their own names,
to the dream,
waiting for its own body,
while all of us prowl the centuries
with our teeth clenched.

> What serves us,
> this clay,
> if it will not drink
> from the river?

PLATO'S CAVE

I keep you
in the cave
of the heart.
There is a fire
and your eyes
are blazing
in the shadow of my hand
on the wall.
I am also afraid
to go out.
What if the sun
has consumed
what I love?

These are my offerings:
Thread of moon
coming down on us
and a handful
of water,
fingers curving
about a river.

How did He
pass breath
into that heavy clay?

And why sing this pain?
Isn't it enough
to persist
in rocking
the emptiness?

ALONE

Sudden,
as the drop of temperature
in the middle of an afternoon,
it's winter,
fast as a gull plunges
toward icy water coming up empty billed.
There's no one to call,
lassitude chills
the habitual energy,
as if under the fire
were ice,
as if the gull broke
its beak on the stone.

There is no antidote
to the stark order of things,
trees planted too far apart to lean,
the wolf alone in his territory,
this galaxy light years from other galaxies,
all the whirling fire of the sky
unable to spark another fire.

What will break open the waters?
Which fisherman will come with his ice sword
to share a circle with an insistent bird?
And is this the only possibility:
        someone waiting,
                alert,
                        harpoon in hand?

BIRD CALLS

In the morning,
it is a small death,
one stone calling
to another
as the heart closes.
If the air shuddered
when the bird plummeted,
no sound was uttered.

This time a claw
scratched the wind
with yellow teeth.
Only bodies want to die. Ghosts
prefer the dark corners,
becoming the snatch
of dream fading
in the morning sun.
This bird
had a song once, now
only this odd plumage
at my feet.

If I say,
I want to die,
it is because
death is so lonely
without us.

THORN

In memoriam, Barbara Myerhoff

Everything dies. Without you
I saw one million flamingos

ignite a lake in Africa.
The same darkness

descended everywhere
when you dropped your body,

I hoped you would tremble
for the beak of God.

Why did we wash you three times
tearing off the girl's white dress

to swaddle you in an austere shroud?
Some say, dying, not death, teaches.

You gained nothing
from that reduction.

Months in the narrow foxhole of disease —
You dug it; we filled it in.

My father is thin as you were
in his hospital bed,

both of you let everything go,
care for nothing

except that barbed hook —
life.

It grabbed you like a thorn
until you begged me, "Pull it out."

❖

Now I consult you daily,
my living oracle,

although you may have fallen again
into this density

or you may have learned nothing.
Even some Buddhist says,

we do not all become fireflies
at the end.

Your absence
in every world

closes the sky.
The birds call in the darkness,

the sunset hidden in feathers,
the sand astir with lice.

WHO KNOWS WHAT THE THIRST IS FOR?
For Barbara

I imagine my own death:
I will want something to drink.

Her buttocks ran like mud.

Her legs were the broken
sticks of the Camps;
she hid them from her sons.

The last day,

She didn't want to see them, or
they couldn't see her
rising like mist.

This life, the chimney.

Whoever cannot imagine Hiroshima
cannot know *oven, shower* or *soap*.

Now her narrow ring
fits the fat finger of my right hand.

A bone was all
Hansel had for protection.

My death will be simple,
I will not be distracted,

I will have had enough practice
to drink the water
and know everything.

DARKENING

The sky suddenly gray,
the world is pewter,
carries the patina
of old things
as metal from the earth
grows upward
into the gallows
of the spirit,
and green
drops away
even into the sea.

Everything hardens
before the coming storm.
We can not say,
it is time stopping,
time readies itself;
the bare sycamore
knows the color of rain,
and in the topmost branch,
unsheltered,
the horned owl,
without hooting,
is certain
of its name.

Hungry
to make a friend
of the universe,
I look for omens and portents,
gather stones,
observe how silently
the roots of trees
are welcomed
into empty veins,
watch the leaf shred
on the glint of mica in rock,
while what I breathe
is crushed
under my feet.

DESERTION

What covers me
in this wilderness
is the rope of night,
this tent of skin.
I surround myself
with nomads,
guides who know the desert
and are lost as well.
They make
a god
of it.

My father is
one of ten tribes
called Wandering,
when there was
nothing,
he named it
One.

In this harsh place,
I touch my lips for salt,
there is no water,
and we are reduced
in all things,
until there is nothing
to honor
but the foot.
Still, I believe in goats
and do not close
my eyes
to the emptiness,
though I am given nothing
but horizons.

Here, I paint dreams
on the sand,
healing the cracks
in my fingers,
while the wind
calls upon the gods
to speak to me
without pity.

SILENCE FOR MY FATHER
For Thich Nhat Hanh and Sister Cao ngoc Phuong

This is the silence around the poem of the death of my father.
This is the silence before the poem.

While my father was dying, the Challenger was exploding on T.V.
Again and again. I watched it happen. In his hospital room,
I followed his breath. And then it stopped.

This is the silence in a poem about the dying of the father.

We're burning the earth and we're burning the sky.

Here is another silence, in the middle of the poem about the
immolation of the Fathers.

The pyres of bodies in Saigon.
The burned air
The charred limbs of dust
The rancid flames
Heat
Light
Fire
                    We turn away.

Shame

Here is another silence within the poem about the burial of the fire.

When my father died, the rains poured down, the moment I picked
up the shovel full of earth. I staggered under the weight of the water.

Another silence please.

I have always wanted to be a woman of fire.
I will have to learn how to rain.
Gently, I will learn how to rain.

I have set fire to your green fields
May I be water to your burning lands.

Please join me in this last silence at the end of the poem of fire.

SOMETIMES AFRAID OF THE IGNOBLE END

Bees in the last honey of the dead hummingbird,
have mercy on us.
Was it always so,
these small and frequent deaths?
I gather the amputated wings,
the deserted nests
and make an altar.
May my dead be with me!
May the candles flutter!
The sky is red and gray
with the rain of feathers,

May there be sweetness
To the last.

CANTA
for Claribel Alegría

In the dream you dream, you hear what the Taoists dream,
the Kabbalists, the shamans, that sound, lost in the universe,
the broken syllables, cacophony calling the great seekers,
to find the signature in bark, in babble,
in the scratch of reeds, slough of water down the slimy rock,
holding the great lost song in its shimmering descent,
the broken syllables of the dumb gods
brooding in the babble, in baboon chatter, in the buzz,

an egg, blue, size of my thumb, broken open, jagged,
a dappled hide, a pictograph of ferns,
might be that vowel, echo of the desperate incantation,
               BERESITH
Need, need, need for a new invocation,
               Let there be light!
against the darkening of blood, the chaos
of the crosshatch of wounds, the turmoil
of broken spines and broken speech,
the apostasies of mutant torturers
the amputations of body and soul,
the...

I'm certain it is only one word, one sound, one breath,
we had it once, Claribel, it was ours,
we lost it, forgot it, it was broken from us,
it's very dark without that word.
Sometimes the poem provides a little light, a match stick
sufficient to continue the search,
but the scratch of the match releases sulfuric recognitions,
the smell of the land burning, human hair crackling in the flames,
indifferent tortures, slavery.

Somewhere in that other country without territory or passports,
the dead are waiting behind the barbed wire of the air,
trying to signal the one word into us,
— they were also deaf when they were here —
they would not recognize the word in the shape of hands,
in the mute arrangement of molecules in the marrow,
in...

The gods say,
we have only to speak it once, only to read it, only to see it,
only...

It's a small thing, we don't, we can't, the wars continue.
Everything is death without that word.
The gods turn aside, having sung once to us,
then out of pity scattered shards of song among the seed pods
for the harvest of the one note.

After the word we will breathe together,
another kind of eloquence,
death only in its own time,
all of us expiring like leaves,
falling in such ruddy gentleness.

Till then, the necessity to speak,
also in sleep,
to speak as if each word might be that cry,
to hold nothing back,
to search the language of every living thing,
also the chant of stones,
a cry every thousand years,
— now, a promise —
even my heart opening as if it were a mouth.

LEAVINGS
For Sister Cao ngoc Phuong

I want what is left:
The tea leaves, the soiled images on cards,
The gasp of words as meaning slips away,
The rinds of the alphabet,
The chewed poems of prisoners,
The bones and the skeletons,
The secretions, the shattered sperm,
The spilled blood,
Broken ova, the phlegm and the cough.

It has always been women's work to prepare the corpse.

But, I will not make a corpse from these elements,
I will make a child.
I will make you such a rose of a child,
A rose of a child held in the crook
Of the dark hand of a dead branch,
I will make you a child shining
Like an angel from these elements of dark,
And the child will sing.

This is what we have
This is what we have to work with.

So give them to me,
First, your dead, moldering
In the dreadful heat of your deserted cities,
Then, give me the iron birds in the sky,
With their demented warbling,
Last, I want your radiant soil
With its eternal shimmer,
Give me everything mangled and bruised,
And I will make a light of it to make you weep,
And we will have rain,
And begin again.

HOW DO YOU KNOW THE BEGGAR AT THE DOOR
IS NOT AN ANGEL?

Dusk silences the stumps of trees,
bricks lie down in this moment
when nothing moves until the breeze
returns, night in its mouth.
Everything is still,
every day has its Sabbath
to cross the river
between earth and gehenna
where the heart of the universe
rests from its interminable pumping.

Here is the dark bird
outside the aorta of night
and a fitful dreamer disappearing in the snow
of a long erotic embrace,
one breath severed from another breath
as the great silence descends,
the beat in utero stilled
against all lamentations.

We could be lost
but Grace assembles
the appetite of wind
to shatter this moment
just edging toward paradise.

The leaves flicker,
the blood scurries once more.
We were so close....

FIRES

In my childhood fevers,
the light that mattered
came from a dark place.
My dreams were blazing with it
before the three houses on the Boardwalk
and Luna Park burned down,
before I watched the fireworks
each Tuesday night.
She carried herself like a torch
at the foot of my bed
in a rain of meteors.

When I could walk alone,
I followed the lighthouse
when the days were short. Later,
the nights were full of fireflies.
My sons caught them
in a mason jar;
it was our lantern.
We went north one summer
where the sun set near midnight,
we took in the light,
drank it like water,
muddied our hands.

The last time I saw her,
the woman in the small box
was luminous,
then we buried her.

SOMETIMES IN CONCERT WITH THE GODS

The sun going down resembled a moon.
Only the faintest scar of gray
crossed the yellow disk.
Heifetz, in the bowl of Turkish mountains,
playing to the nightingales,
was answered, song for song.
Memories are the miner's light,
the yellow birds carried
into the dark shaft
to keep us safe.
The sun fell into the blue mountain,
the mountain opened and swallowed the sun,
yellow as the rising moon.

The first day,
the acacia was a light in the room,
but then it dried,
the insistent yellow,
from a distance, seemed the same,
but, standing next to the tree,
I saw the light inside was gone.
Within the week she died,
the tree fell down.

At eight, in a fever,
I dreamed a stairway of light,
yellow rabbits on my bed, and God.
Steam in the black iron pot
on the gas flames,
cobalt blue and cadmium yellow,
ochre, saffron, lemon, xanthous, chrome.

At the end of the street,
beyond the gate house
and the barbed wire,
and before the black breakwater,
was the lighthouse;
we were never without light.
We lived on a point of land,
a sandy sliver
jutting into the dark straits.
Memories streaking down my back
in yellow chalk.

At Sounion, the sea
put on the clothes of the sun,
was all gold and amber,
was light itself.
Then the sun vanished,
the sea had eaten it
for the dark.
Last birds flew over
in a blue sweep, singing.
Poseidon had been there
for thousands of years
and his temple fallen down.

PRIESTS AND MAGICIANS

Priests are the intermediaries between people and gods; magicians
serve as the intermediaries between gods and people. The
penetration of the realms of the visible and invisible makes it
possible for everything to be set right.
I Ching, Wilhelm/Baynes edition, Book III: The commentaries, 57, Sun, The Gentle

In the Beginning
We were one animal,
One breathing for the day
And the other breathing for the night,
Or we were Leviathan
Her tail in Her mouth
About His great golden egg,
Or, before that division,
We were the world tree, breathing
Day and night in succession,
An oak door opening and closing,
Later we were priestess and magician,
Climbing
Into the songs of God.

Then, after the sunrise,
We fell,
As a star falls,
As Lucifer,
As Lilith,
As night falls
As cadence falls
As prayer falls,
As rain,
   as snow,
     as water
       fall,

     Full of light.

31

ENDARKENING

If darkness
— black ice of the universe —
punctured the day sky,
— coal needles piercing
the blue numinous air —
if the Northern Darks
were the sacred fingers of noon
and a black rain fell
— dusty and iridescent —
on my lover's black hair
and all the crows and ravens...

Could we love the light less?
Could we learn to explode the darkness?
Then the death of slow ashes
would cover us quietly,
and this terrible white fire
would not last forever
in our banked radiant bones.

SPARKS

Ignorant
of the letters of god,
I dreamed of painting the morning,
while every day,
the signature of fire
falls like rain.

Where are we?
How have we entered here?

And the way back?
A long climb to night
as onto the back of air.

THAT WOMAN IS TALKING TO HERSELF

Lost this morning,
in the gale
as the rain is lost in it.
I know this wind
with my eyes closed.
These fingers wizened
with the alphabet of the deaf
grasp at the invisible,
while I go forth
only with a faith in rope.
Things held in place,
the gods pulling on us,
at each hand,
the tether is
the morning star.

My elbows say,
brace yourself in ribs
while the feet
of the universe
run from each other.
Going abroad,
I hunt the streets
of the moon,
bemoaning the only voice,
wind,
and the duet in my throat.

And everywhere, the gods
speaking through the holes
in my coat.

ATOMIZED

You call it
the cosmic dance,
these pieces of us
in everything else,
but it's a way
of being lost
with no one
searching for me
but myself
and I,
without feet.

Hold me,
to know
the shape of my shoulders,
to recognize
my bones
buried
where the wind
arches
over a hill.

What remains
of me
is a fierce shadow,
while leaves
mend
in the green air.

I climbed
the mountain face
before
the invention of ropes,
remembering
we made a chair
of four hands,
but,
I was a child.

THE TREES ASK ME HOME

    soon
I'll sleep each night
with the breath of leaves
in the bed, the cough of eucalyptus,
the restless stirring of fig and lime.
There is so much life here,
rooster as alarm, hawk as sentinel,
coyote as guard; there is so much life
and ferment, death is close by.

When the human species deserted him,
tomatoes were what my father planted,
they were his true love.
With their imperative, he spent
weekends in the sun.
So I learned to talk to trees.
I see the song coming, a wing
out of the nest of bitterness,
light and dark. And further on,
those footsteps in the mulch
and that path through the new grove,
must be mine.

    It seems
the story of my life
is the story of trees I've loved,
some are standing, some fell down.

UNDER THE SORROW TREE

By the river,
under the sorrow tree,
the universe says
the bones must dance,
and she, who goes out with a net
to catch the spirits,
returns, her hands filled
only with the dark briars
we have hummed
these many years.
The one who sees sorrow
can not staunch it,
yet by her side
something white
announces itself.
The bones are sucked clean,
the one nearest the heart
becomes a flute,
when you blow,
the dead come
and behind them,
the other bones in a circle

The universe says
loss demands birth
and the two
are lovers.

THE MIRACLE
For Naomi

These
cracked
vessels
hold
water.

TEPHERET

WALLS

All day long I create a bulwark. I gather the living along with the dead and build a wall. Each soul is a stone for the last days. I am like Lot. I need to gather a city of souls to rebuke the God of fire.

There is a problem: these souls have to live in the heart. The heart expands, infinitely it seems, while my body thins according with the thinning of time. Perhaps I become a grotesque with an enlarged heart visibly ticking within my chest like a boy whose head is larger than his body can sustain.

This is my work. Men have built walls before but they were thinking of war. When I say we are stones, I am a woman who means that we fit against each other, that we breathe slowly, that we have been here from the beginning, that we can not be burned. And when the Lord of Fire comes and wants fifty souls, there will be fifty souls. We will stand up to Him. No one will be destroyed.

MAYBE A BROTHER IS ADDRESSING HIS SISTER

This desert,
these forty years,
this age,
this rock, struck
by this hand,
after the manna
after all the miracles
the tablets and
the revelations,
still, this fall,
this forgetting.

I can see it,
all green
and flowing milk,

So, I ask you,
serpent tongue,
take me
into your cursed body,
you madwoman,
leper, you seer,
you carry me,
this man,
hunch on your back,
to honey.

HERESY

In the coldest climate,
I will survive,
my bones
burning
like the
burning
bush.

EXODUS

When the sea opens red,
froth at the farthest shore,
salty lips stretch open
between mountainous thighs and sands.
You have crossed safely,
take off your shoes,
those in chariots will drown.
Comets shake the air,
the earth heaves
the quickening sand,
there is brine on your mouth.
She promises manna,
rain from the teats
in the sky,
curd of the white sperm milk.
You survive on belief,
the desert devours all,
those who have walked on water
will walk in fire.

SHABBAT

A city
beneath a city,
every hill
is a graveyard,
beneath the grass
a continuous sabbath.

When you walk here,
you burn your feet
on candle flames.

BREAKING GROUND

Toward the south, through the center
of a still brown patch of weeds,
a living green line,
like marble dividing stone,
cuts the hill, a caesarean section
from navel to pubic bone.
Scar on the belly of my mother
where I tore her open.
Across the canyon, a rock face
has been split into labia
and there are hundreds of buttocks and hips,
breasts cut with a water knife
from the body rock.

Here is the winter knot
before it's cut into spring.
In my belly,
the stone of light
split open,
something green emerged
and exploded into a thousand arms.

The grass has come again,
insidious spring over the disguised rock,
the mustard returns and the lupine bruise
in the raw, scabrous wind,
now acacia, bees, moths, ants, birds
ground out of uterine stone.

This is the order:
green, earth, stone, sulphur, bedrock, fire.

    Peace and trembling
    throughout the body of the Mother.

TRESPASSING

The river gets to the sea. The mouth opens.
There's a word for it. *Embouchure.* Think
of a french whore. I'd like to change my profession
now that my poems are wide and the flute is in them.

I slip into an easy chair. The muscles pull
into a new shape. The wind freshens, changes direction,
the sun is falling into the sea, apricot tree spilling
its branches toward the ground. I stuff my mouth
with cherries, enter the house, drop my dress on the floor.
The shoes are under the bed, the bougainvillea gains
the top of the wall and falls over, begins to grow down,
mango seed pressed against the tongue, the planets
tug at all the branches. This round of living
may be done with the eyes closed.

Everything is a piece of a circle,
but there must also be doors in it. The Navajo
leave a thread for the spirit to cross over.
The stream has a trunk across it. Nothing stands by itself.
The wall is perforated, water always burrows somewhere,
is not interested in fences. When the rain falls,
enterprising men put up stakes in the puddles:
"This rain is mine."
Sweat is a double virtue— salt and water.
Here's a June flood. The butterfly trespasses,
the squirrel rides the tree in the wind, the jay
squawks and steals, the locust has no respect for boundaries,
the sun, mercilessly, bears down,
water rising and the dust as well.

Everything we have
is the gift of one of the four directions.

OWL
For Michael Ortiz Hill

For my birthday, you give me the wing of a dead owl to sit beside the wing of another. My Cherokee friend said, "Owl can be dangerous." It can cause the air to turn black as the path of Owl streaking toward a mouse. It can cast spells for years after its death. Indians say, "Owl is strong medicine." I tried to teach the black cat, Hecate, what no mother cat had taught her, shook her in the air when the mating owls hooted; it was not sufficient. She disappeared on Halloween the night after I'd held her in my arms, looking in her yellow eyes, saying, "We are strange companions." Hecate, like Lilith, is the owl goddess, the goddess of crossroads, of caves and dark places. The gods in all their forms take themselves back, again and again into themselves. You found the wing on the road, among other wings. On my altar, I put what had to have been mutilated by a man. I take a chance. Trust is one of the trials of the dharma.

On your birthday, Owl is sentinel over the darkening meadow. You are the one to spy its silhouette against the sky, a practice you developed as a child. We sit on stones staring in different directions. This small circle might also mark the rise of sun or moon. In our calendars, this is the end of the first year we have known each other. We have been given the task of loving with every conscious breath. It does not matter that the owl does not answer our calls when we hoot to it. The *who* of the female is lower than the *who* of the male. We know this from the sound of our voices. After six months, the wing you gave me is living in the meadow.

THE TAMING POWER OF THE SMALL

I am sharing my house with one or another species. No one knocks. No one comes through the door. There is my bed and a series of nests. The rat stole a towel, then a sock, made a house of cotton, eating at it at night.

What does the cricket eat? The ants want sugar and the bees want honey to make honey like love which feeds on love.

There's a lizard between the books and squirrels under and over the house. Creatures I can not name spin webs, crusade across the floor. I said I came to live alone.

Before dawn, the rooster crows and Timber Wolf responds in his long eloquent howl. I learn another kind of talk. What does the spider write on my skin as I sleep? And the song of the cricket, what does it mean?

Only the hills don't move except for the occasional yawn and stretch of the slow life of stones turning under my feet in their rocky sleep remembering ancient eruptions in air of magma dreams.

Everywhere my eyes rest, something is scratching and scampering. The slither, the slide, spy and strike, stalk and sting. All these creatures sing as they go about the mating, the play and the kill.

The wolf and I feed fleas before we die. I can't hear their cry, but some people say you can teach them to dance. As the elm has beetles, the jays come to feast. The quails graze on the rye as they arrive at twilight in a long parade through the tall, dry grass.

If my heart opens, what will nest in it? What will come in through its cracks and screens with the dust and flies? What will slip over its threshold and under its door? What will bore through its walls?

If I open the door, what creature on his two legs will enter and how long will he stay? What will he eat? Will he, like the smaller ones, say in his own odd language: This is my home. I will live here.

REVOLUTION (MOLTING)

The man's in the shower and the slow, heavy blood is in me. The dawn comes in dark, comes in with the barometer falling and the pressure of air swirling as it funnels down to the water.

I am dropping through this place of silence, only a drop of water in the vortex of wind, edging through vertical turns to the sweat that becomes the sea. It is too difficult to think of trees.

Outside, there is the world, but I can't see it through the window. The phone rings. Someone is at the door. On the radio, they speak of hurricanes, giving them human names, pretending they come on feet.

My blood says, "I am the weather." Water runs down the back of the house. The humidity increases. The mirrors fog so we can't see our faces.

I mourn the absence of the bitch, the certainty of her sleep, how she lay on her back, paws falling to the side, her belly exposed.

If I were a reptile, if I were the snake I killed, if I were any of a thousand, slow creatures, I would know. But I am a woman, given to wearing language as I wear a hat, a dress, a pair of underpants, a bit of scent.

I want to be naked. But naked under the skin. Naked under the bones, under, in the swirl, in the hollow that the winds make, there in the funnel of my body, naked in the moment and in the precipitation.

WORK ON WHAT HAS BEEN SPOILED

Morning finds the lines on my face. I do not pull the curtains against the new light. No things look in but squirrels, the century plant and quail. I do not lock the gate and can not lock the house. Fences invite danger, or nothing can keep out a determined evil. Defenseless, I rely on my wolf, the elements and the green at the end of the knoll.

The man with the gun said, "Guns bring guns." He wants to live at the edge of the land under the trees he planted. He wants to talk to leaves. When he was riding the tractor, watching out for water lines, he remembered Vietnam, watching for mines. But the death here is the natural death of the season. The priority is the life of the tree, is the coming of fruit, is the green food.

I can not say, "My hands are clean." I can not say, "I have not killed."

Even yesterday, squashing the persistent bugs between my thumb and index finger, I imposed gratuitous death. We could have co-existed.

And I killed the dog. "Hecate," I called her, for her barnacles and red eyes, for her female age. I sent her to the underworld after a seven week reprieve.

I have killed three creatures this year: the rattler stretched across the threshold of my house, Hecate and the rat. And in return I plant the olive, the redwood and the pine.

Here is the balance: We are always between our birth and our dying. Silk of the grey of your hair, softening of skin, lines at the corner of your eyes. Like mine. Like mine.

COMING TO MEET

Animals live in the house, nest in the roof, lair under the floor, the bricks collapse, roots enter, the walls tilt. Every small creature takes us down to the tiny labyrinth.

Wherever I walk, the living scurry about the bones of the dead, ghosts streak fog across the windows. The cock crows. Eggs, brown and hot, bulge onto the straw.

This living continent heaves like a man tossing in his bed, dream damp about his temples, a stained sheet wrapped, knowingly, about his chest.

Why do you enter me with so much flesh? You come to me swelling with the dream of the porpoise.

There was a pool under the house where the mysterious creature twisted in a whirlpool of water. "Give it to the sea," someone shouted, and the pool opened as wide as my body, but the porpoise was lonely and stayed behind. We gathered it, as one gathers water, into a smaller nest.

Last night we hung our hammocks in the trees, one hammock next to another, aligned like private beds or graves, each in its own dark. I lean into you now, trying to drown or breathe under water. Your breath is my breath. I say to myself, "Enter this bed of water."

Who are you? Are you the light or the darkness, the air or the water, the earth or the underworld, the living body or the dying?

SHEILA AND I WATCH THE SUNSET
TURN RED AND GRAY
For Sheila

A thousand shades of gray
prepare me for old age.
Color fading
as we list toward the poles,
ice carrying us slowly
to the final snow, but

peppers today,
red and burning
against the glacial feet.

THAT PHILOSOPHICAL SADNESS
THAT COMES DOWN IN THE DAWN

is a guest
singing, invisible,
in my body.
It takes so long
to speak without words,
to still the breast
in its milk song.
Each of us abed
in our long loneliness,
can not pretend
the centaur or the sphinx,
only the intermittent
dream or nightmare
makes us one.

If I once saw
the mating of the mermaids
in the spouting ocean
where the great dolphin
thresh their salty wheat,
I have forgotten it.

How do I know
when the heart opens,
if it is love or emptiness?
It's only a door opening
and someone comes in
or exits.

Still, it is a door,
with a singing guest,
coming and going.

I WROTE MY LOVER A LETTER WITHOUT WORDS

I said,
I am a small woman,
bold enough to want
to hold a planet in my broken heart.

I said,
Here stillness falls
upon the shoulder of stillness,
as one shadow disappears in another.
Everything is here
in the point of this moment of air.

I said,
Under this hand of silence,
this woman comes to life,
like a waterfall undressing itself.

I said,
Reduced to a needle of light,
I am completely myself.

I said,
In each moment,
the story of the universe is repeated:
There was nothing.
Look what is coming to be.
You always surprise me.

HOW IT IS

Earth breathing,
Two cradles,
I swing in you,
you swing in me.
This holding
        tree
    in the wind,
moves the beloved.

GATHAS

AWAKENING GATHA

Waking in the morning
Time smiles in my hand.
This dawn
Lasts all day.

AWAKENING GATHA

Waking in the morning:
May I be awake.

AWAKENING GATHA

This bell
And this morning,
My life calling
To my life.

DEATH GATHA

Skull of a mare
In the arm of a tree.
May we be lovers
In the end.

THE RIVER DOES NOT TURN ON ITSELF
for Lisa Klein

The sieve asks
to marry the river,
the spirits say,
it belongs to the bank,
this old earth
knows how to move
the shoulder of water
without loss.
The jug takes the river
to her mouth,
she has lived through fire
and cooled in leaves.

The river goes
where it must,
it can not linger
in these bare hands,
the spirits follow
the river,
and the drawer of water
must fashion her bucket
from bone.

CARRIER PIGEONS

The birds come fluttering,
then vanish. I say,
they are love letters
from you, assuming
the interconnectedness
of all things.
You say, there is nothing
mythic about love or the loss
of it. You say,
it has happened before
and again. You say,
the moon is a lamp post,
stones do not speak,
nothing pulls at us, but
our death.

But, sometimes,
not alone in the universe,
I receive heralds
and sentinels.

This afternoon in the hills,
your breath in the wind,
the alphabet of wings
our lives warming
in the feathers.

Oh, my love,
so far away,
how sweet the air.

NUPTIALS

That afternoon,
knee deep in leaves
before the autumn burning,
scattering what ripens,
what falls, what dies,
we traced
the secret ribs and veins
rising with the water in the tree,
until our holy vows
were in the sky,
the clouds,
also drifting, orange,
everything flaming.

Then loss was not age,
was not the leaf song
under our feet,
we were the new hearth fire.
Still, we were pulled apart,
even as branches
set out
for the four directions.

We were six,
at that wedding of children,
we were the morning.
Now, I want something else
from the tree,
not innocence,
but perfect knowledge
knee deep in leaves,
bending toward holy matrimony
in the beginning of each year.

WILD

That night cry
of a woman in the hills
is only a cougar,
the shadow
in the heart of the meadow
is the bobcat, awake.
That slouch of fur amidst
the stammering of trees
is the wild
coming down
to my palm, at last.

KETHER

THE BUDDHA OF THE BEASTS
for my son, Greg, and also Timber Wolf

You arrived after howling alone for days. At first, companion to the other wolf, you lived in the animal realm and busied yourself with that domestic life. Then at the moment when you lost your mate, we found your territory. Perhaps you are the only and the last wolf to wander in such hills.

You are the gift from my son. Your presence breaks that silence between us. You are everything we can not speak about, but he has always known my longing for the wild thing is greater than my fear.

Three times when I walked to the river, at dusk, I broke the spider net gleaming over the path between the two trees. We call you the Buddha Wolf, watching the play of light as you bound between the worlds.

This is what I know about you: I can not break your will. You will not be alone and you must be free. You are absolute and generous about your territory. The howl is more than an acknowledgement of the Moon. Every living thing, but one, is fluent in the language of the Great Heart.

It is a half mile downhill through the dark shade of the second growth redwoods to the river. After a hundred and fifty years, the grove which was desecrated is somewhat restored. There has been time for timbers to fall and for the sycamore, pine, laurel to turn about each other. Of course, what had been there for centuries is now present only in the wind, in the great shadow of the invisible limb toward which we are all climbing.

Now when I come to the river, the Great Blue Heron is waiting. He walks upstream while I follow in his rhythm along the path. I say the names of the animals, not to separate myself, but as one repeats a rosary of preservation.

I liberate a self like one carves a stone, I excavate it from a garbage dump, from the detritus of culture, from the axe of expectation, from demand and sorrow. This unexpected self emerges from that compost like a sapling from the rotting stump of an old redwood. Even as I age, there is something in me becoming a girl. A stump that was cut down, flourishes again.

The first dog I ever had was a wanderer, came home smelling of fish oil, rotting food, covered with muck. I did not dare follow him then. You are old. Sometimes in the damp winters you limp. The hip is slow. It is an effort for your lungs to take in the breath and let it go. Still there is a deepening circle of light around your arcane silence, you gather it to you the way the trees I love gather the night. I always wonder how a Buddha Wolf will die.

In the order of things, it is easier for the gods to live in a tree or in a four legged creature than in a person. The living child goddess of India presides in terrible silence until she bleeds and then she's thrown into this life the way a carcass is thrown to the wolves. Even though it begins as a child, still the gods can not take hold in the stink where the men have put their paws.

We can only heal so much. Some of what is broken in me will always be broken. Some grief is irreparable. You will die with or without a flash of lightning. The thousand year old trees will not return in the lifetimes of my species.

Still, I did not expect that ultimately you would be my mate. The girl I was did not guess she would become the gray wild-haired witch of the hill. Speaking the languages of beasts and trees was not how I had imagined my life.

WHEN THEY ALL PAINTED FOR THE GODS
For Jane

The god comes,
invisible feathers
brushing against
your morning thigh.
There's only color
and a heart
beating
in your heart.
The brush
in your hand
knows the god,
follows
the shadow
on the page,
a footprint
in the sand
where no one
has been.

The hours
of the sun
rising
every
day.

EAVESDROPPING IN THE MORNING

Two empty chairs
face each other
under the bower of the old elm,
each year branches break off
from the weight of water drawn up.
I can see the gods, cross-legged,
chatting in the morning green light.
Soon the beetles will hatch
and devour the leaves
on this divine scaffold
but now the extended branches
are green.

    Question:
        How do I keep my eyes open,
        my mouth in the shape of prayer,
        and something under my ass?

COSMOLOGY

There is no difference
    tree or fire,
the burning to leaf in the mid-day light
or the night sun,
        that black crow
flying with flames in its beak,
when the long hair of the little moon
casts itself down in roots of light.
A great green net holds us all.

The heat of my breath warms the universe,
    two old stones rubbed together
in the marriage bed,
tell the entire story.

THE TREE IS THROWN INTO THE LIGHT

for Steven Kent and Nancy Bacal

The tree is thrown into the light
the remaining leaves at the branch tips
rush forward like arrows
as the luminous sap
speeds shining up the trunk.

Last night returning from the mountains,
other last leaves caught the last sun
and glowed in ambush for us
as we descended.
Losing the light, we lost color,
but turned at the edge of night,
and found the deep blues,
grays and inky greens in the chaparral,
the spectrum of the dark.
'Any light, any light,' we thought.

We'd managed to climb the ridge
into the last feet of light,
I wonder if we held it then
as the tree holds it now,
or if the light merely fell on us
until our shadows fell into the dark.
When the sun slid away from us,
we came down shivering, gratified.

The tree is bare, the limbs
bend into the light in windy ecstasy,
when the dark comes suddenly, the tree
will glower like a splintered moon.
I've come to the same dark so often
dreaming of the burning bush,
embers and salamanders.
Years I've tried to learn the secret
of raising the fearful mercury
in a glass body
learning to hold
whatever heat and light there is,
knowing, this winter, this matters so much.

WATCHING MICHAEL ROAR

I
You run fast,
your great horns
bruise the adamant bark,
sparks fly through the trees,
the stones catch fire
and the rain
which extinguishes all,
descends through your fists
of white ecstatic light.

II
This fire
has nothing to burn
until we're broken
and offer
these chars to lick.
Fire has a mouth
which is unequalled.

III
Grief, my love,
then shattering,
and then the heart,
crawling like a living thing,
hungry and naked.

IV

The exultant stretch
of your invisible neck,
your transparent mouth
open and singing,
your body
trembling in the void.
I have no words when I see
the gods descending
into our two bodies.

V

Cornea of stars,
chest of helium,
great stellar nitrogen shriek
of song,
you reach up,
lightning rod,
and pull everything down.

VI

You wanted ashes?
Here is the hoof print
of god upon your temple
and some embers, burning
like thorns,
in my mouth.

VII

Feathers singed,
my little angel,
and your wings dark
with fire,
the brand of your lips
on my breastbone.
When you cried out,
I saw the flame,
soot falling
onto my eyes.

VIII

Angel,
light of your wings,
burns.
Fire
is easier, it
can be put out.

IX

I've seen you ride
this two headed beast,
four legs to make
one body, flank
galloping on flank,
trembling and rearing,
and the rider
thrown
into the stars.

SWING

Earth breathing,
two cradles,
I swing in you,
you swing in me.
This holding
    tree
in the wind,

Which is the beloved?

RUMINATIONS

For Michael
by Deena Metzger

For Deena
by Michael Ortiz Hill

After months of planning
I finally met you
by accident.

Now that we love each other
I am afraid
When I conjured love,
I had no fear.
As before God,
I dedicate myself,
but afterwards,
in The Presence,
I am afraid.

The night before we met
I dreamt you were a giantess
with two singing daughters
Next morning, I found
you would fit well under my arm
[the proverbial dove]
that your voice was from Brooklyn
and very very soft.

There is nowhere to go after this,
I am accustomed to running forward or away
And this morning,
in the midst of a dry summer,
it rained.

I said, "In my heart of hearts
I want to know you as a lover."
You didn't answer.
I could have died in your silence.
I said, " I am not carrying
a concealed blade."
And for a second you held belief and disbelief
in a wry smile.

When you touch me,
I can not tell
      if you are taking something
      or making an offering.

                  Then the Buddhists came
      and planted a small monument for peace
      right in the middle of our conversation.
      The little Japanese girl refused to nibble
                  the wild fennel
                  I had picked for her.

        Bright orange phallus parting
             the labia of a mussel
             in the Italian restaurant,
             the century plant blooms
             once every hundred years.
                  If it's not one thing
                  it's another.

No matter whom else you meet
in this world
even after I die,
I am the one.
That is what is so surprising:
we planned this,
only the bodies and lives
have been given to us.
Now we must undress,
it is more fearful since
it isn't the first time,
and it is.
I've done this so many times with you,
that is why I'm always forgetting.

                  I never met someone
             I more enjoy giving gifts to.
         I've always wanted to love you well.
        This is the dharma I cannot betray.

Because I belong to you,
I know you can never leave me,
if there isn't this life,
there's the next one,
and there's always
the first one
which neither of us
can leave.

The first summer I loved you,
I could not stop touching
the absence of your breast.
This pale body loved your dark skin,
this young boy liked to trace his fingers
along the wrinkles near your eyes.

Last night in your sleep,
despite our vow of silence,
you spoke to me
of mundane matters,
like your love for me.

Under arrest in Honduras
the frightened boy with his gun
slung over his shoulder
shouting at me,
I reminded myself
"Just one more border to cross
and I will be in the arms of my lover."
When I am not with you for a long time
I get a little crazy,
I never could forgive the Sandinistas
that you were so far away.

How will you know,
when you enter,
that this time,
I have no clothes on at all?
See how ruthless my love is?
I will also strip you
down to the bone,
even you,
with all your fashions and pretendings.

The old man
with his burlap sack of pine needles
made for us an altar,
a new kind of crèche
at the foot of the volcano.

Now you want me
to go back
to the old life,
as if after meeting God,
one is still applying
to a dating service.

You thought I couldn't see
the light and shadow
of the ancient city
nor hear our footfalls
on the cobbled streets.

A haze of blue smoke
over the village
in the morning of tortillas.

Firecrackers at midnight
like a hailstorm on a tin roof—
I was inside of you
when the New Year began.

In this life, then,
I love you,
this face, this body,
this life of yours.
You're such a poor man,
you have no others.

I wanted to write a poem
about thinking about you all the time,
"a glass of wine long after moonrise
thinking of you,"
"springtime of narcissus in the dusty alley
walking all by myself
thinking of you,"
but such a poem
could have no natural end.

I do not know
how to reach you
except through these bodies
we must take off
again and again.
Rumi says,
"I want to kiss you,
the price of kissing is your life."*

*from Open Secrets, Versions of Rumi, *by John Moyne and Coleman Bark,*
Threshold Books, Putney, Vermont, 1984

NO WORDS FOR RUMI

Silence pours into me
as a cataract of wine
overflowing the sides
of a glass chasm.
If I do not speak
I will die.
If I speak
this silence
which has become my breath
will disappear.
How can I pretend
these are not words
or how can I speak
when I am drinking
and under water?

And the order of things,
the wine flooding
down the mountain,
it is so sweet
I fear
there is no end to it.

BURNING THE NIGHT

Lightning tears the heart the way the air is seared, then sealed, when the Gods descend. Did you think The Presence would fail to leave a scar?

The tree joyous with the instant of being set alight, is a great torch. Everyone knowing the chosen one by the roar of living gold, by the plume of smoke, bends toward it. Sometimes an entire forest taken down. Trees humbled but grateful for the holy flame.

Come then to the ones who endure, and ask wisdom from the charred cunt, from the dark burned cave at the root, where the Gods forged their knowledge. This, they said, is the lovemaking: "Beware."

So we go to each other hoping to die but also afraid.
That is
Hoping to burn
That is
Hoping to hold the fire.

To be the lightning rod of air, to blaze first with the invisible platinum stamens of stars, then to be a doorway, afterwards and for all time, through which the fierce hunger for the body enters the nest of emptiness which has become ourselves.

Is that what you want?

HERONS, THE SHADOWS THEY CAST

Coming to the water, at last, I listen to the one note of the bird squawking in the redwoods across the river. I sit on the sand along the bank without putting my feet in the water.

A man in white trunks enters the river. I can not keep myself from wondering if he killed someone in Vietnam. He is the right age, lifts weights, even now arranges boulders to form a step, so we know he lets nothing alone, neither his body nor the river. But when he swims finally, he does the breast stroke which doesn't take him anywhere, only keeps him afloat. So I assume, he hasn't killed anyone with his hands.

The stones I lean against on this quiet beach are as white as the tooth of the bobcat who lives near my house. The grey shadow the beast casts as it hunts carries a certain darkness of its own. There is another shadow on the snippet of stoney sand bar, the color of blueberries, dark blood, as if the night stretched itself out for an early nap before sundown.

What else is possible in the river which would wash the hunter and the lonely woman alike? I have not killed a man, or a woman, to my knowledge. And in this moment, I am not lonely, except for someone I dreamed my life was becoming and this one I did kill.

"How?" you ask.
By not coming to the river, perhaps.
By speaking too soon or too late.
By thinking there is more than the song of birds.
By how carefully I choose to live my life.

Soon the shadow is deeper and not as blue. The bobcat of my imagination has moved on, but the dark remains, because he is a hunter all his life, even asleep, and, therefore, leaves his mark.

And now, a great heron, feathers some color of blueberries, arcs down to the water. The blue sky, on its own, mates with no one, can be entered and exited, never scars, holds everything and nothing. The bird that fell out of it, color of sky and shade, was hunting in the river for fish.

The woman I was supposed to be, that dead one, sees this and her heart breaks, also, before she vanishes again. Nothing can heal this loneliness for the dead, not even suicide.

We say shadows are blue. The sky and the improbable blueberries and the jays are blue, even the hedge of flax and lupine against the white wall, the hydrangeas, the lilies of the Nile, all of these are indeed blue. But the Great Blue Heron as it glides by me now in a straight line, confident in the existence of air, following the river, which is blue, to the ocean, also blue, this heron, is now gray, like the shadow on the sandbar, like the rocks against my back, gray as everything that lasts.

The loneliness of the species for its true self, for the blue of sky inside the tabernacle of mind, for the Nile flowers, water pulling itself out of the river into a mirror of petals, the bouquets of the bank, the muddy cloisters where the herons, egrets, cranes, sequester themselves among the wet reeds, this longing for the sharp and precise bill with which to pluck a just and simple meal out of the water, for the descent of empty blue sky, the astonishing blue eye of wisdom, is easy to bear and as natural as the stains of all the varieties of blue berries, which ripen toward our mouth. I bear this loneliness as a great gift. Memory, even of loss, brings possibility closer.

But there is another loneliness which is not blue but is the color of the smudged sky or the pulverized rock, which has no birth in the blue or green or gold of natural things, this loneliness is born whenever we murder another or ourselves. And this loneliness can not be borne and never subsides. This is the loneliness of the woman who will no longer go into the river.

BECOME ONE WITH ME

A silence grows somewhere about my heart. It is the silence between all the words. It enters the way lovers are surprised by each body vanishing in the other.

I open my mouth. Breath enters, filling the loneliness. If I were to decide to die, I would remain part of the earth. There is no way to escape the bond. Even a capsule with dead men will not circle the earth endlessly. They will be pulled down to the soil. I could not pull away from the earth if that were necessary to save it.

In a poor country, my friend sits with the pistol he shares with his wife upon his lap. The small man with a limp used to be a dancer. The bombs from my country are falling nearby, silver as rain. Alongside the beans and coffee, he is growing orchids. What is it you would like me to say?

This silence when the words are falling away. Also, I do not know if I can manage the larger silence which they say saves something.

Finches mating in the wedding baskets under the eaves. The one with the red throat flutters on the back of the downy one. A seed is passed from beak to beak. A twig in the mouth or a bit of fur. Long, fine silk hairs braided into the chalky scat on the trail. Sometimes a bobcat prowls by my window toward the hills. Flowers, still wild, small and scattered like snow.

From out of a mire of leaves on the copper of madrone laurel, the triumphant sprint of a single flowering peach twig announces itself. I spend the day releasing it from the confinement of passionate branches wondering, 'Do I have the right to strike down the wild thing for the domestic fruit?'

A woman in a car parked at the edge of the fragrant sage speaks. "I play God," she says to no one at all, "and God plays the chord." There is the sound of a wooden flute, I think.

The trees poison me with their touch. The sap insists itself under my skin, wants me to carry it. I can only bemoan the density of my body which flares at the necessary intermingling of species. This penetration burns. There is nothing to be done for it but to cover myself with clay, to bury myself in earth.

"Neither hot nor cold can pass this point," says the sutra. Nothing which is itself can pass over the river. Anything which is so completely itself, is partial, is only itself, is not another, is a broken thing, is halved, or even less, is only a fragment, is like the flower which the bomb has exploded. Anything which is completely itself can never be whole.

There is something in a word. I can hear it now. Something other than the ordering of one word after another, something other than the meaning or the song, something else. Something in the word itself. Or rather when it sits next to another word, something there, two lovers on a bench, that secret. Then the words open their musk and the net is visible. Everything is caught.

The war thinks it can be one by itself. The war thinks it can be won by itself. The war cuts itself into pieces. It whittles itself down. When we all disappear, it will be so much itself, it will be so large, there will be nothing left of it. Without me, the war is only a splinter and that itself broken. It will be by itself, like a dry husk, on the disappearing side of the dry river.

Each spring for seven years now, the owls call to each other all night in slow and leisurely conversation. Suddenly, I hear a rapid trill of two voices at once. I bless their mating in the dark, the quick duet. And now the singing again, and the time it takes to formulate the question and then the answer.

I am saying the name of my friend. I am saying it again and again. I am saying it like a rosary or a cord of amber beads, or a mantra of jade, or the fringe on a tallith, or a necklace of turquoise and silver coins, or a prayer wheel loose in the wind. I am turning the hour and the day and the year on the axis of his name. I am watching the earth spin on the point of the sacred alphabet of his name. I am spinning the bombs away. I am spinning them faster than light. I am spinning the silver of bombs into a thread of light which can not disappear us. As long as I remember my friend, he will stay alive.

So I marry you again and again. I want to become one with you. I can hear the silence in the silence coming like a wild storm. It is falling upon us. The world is a great knot and we are tied into it, one into the other. Here the word is singing itself into being on this other side of the living waters of the river.

LOOKING FOR THE FACES OF GOD

Seemingly endless eddies in the descent of the river. Eternity, they say, in the running water. Trees thousands of years old and still springing up again from their fallen trunks in ceaseless regeneration. The forest is deep. I have been sitting here at the edge waiting for the blessing of an occasional glimpse of the other side of the river.

In the heart is a small mirror which must be pierced in order to see the faces of God. It is behind an oak door which can only be opened with the key which is inside the golden egg within the rare singing bird nesting atop the highest tree on the unscalable peak of the remote mountain where the water begins. Take me there.

From the road, when I first looked down, I thought I saw water, but I was looking at a river of dry stones, and beside it the rivulet hugging the farthest bank. Here we sat all afternoon learning to read the wind.

I know the secret: If we sit here and do not move, do nothing, the river will fill with water and the dry stones will no longer shatter in the sun. If we sit here and do not speak of anything we know, the door will open on its own accord, as simply as a reed is moved aside by the breeze or a vine lifts rocks to its own twisted bosom.

The first day we didn't speak, the skunk came nosing along the bank. Graceful and industrious, it ambled about without concern for our shadows stretching toward the woods in the setting sun.

Prayer for the setting of the sun: Thank you for this day. Thank you for my life. May we live in the spirit and the heart. May we be Your lyre.

I want you to know my heart is broken. But not broken enough.

Trompe l'oeil. I thought I had opened the door of the heart but I had only painted an opening.

The climb up the mountain, the test, the ordeal, the suffering, the cold, fatigue and deprivation, the studying and chanting, the persistent quest, the fever and fasting, have only one purpose: to open the eye of the heart.

On the second day, we found a lagoon downriver. We could see farther into the trees. The light was golden there and the black terns cavorted in the soft grasses at the bank. We said nothing to each other all day long.

It occurred to me I was ashamed to love God. It was as difficult for me to love God as it was for me to love a beggar. Two days before, I had dreamed the Bomb had been dropped in the far North. We could no longer stay in the room of windows and unbearably clear light. The deadly, invisible poison arrived without warning, or, in the beginning without affect.

I am not certain there is no life in stones. I am not certain that the trunk askew on the hillside is not a great green horned praying mantis in the night. I am not certain that the root burl torn out of the earth is not the Medusa or a giant boar.

On the third day we were swimming upstream toward our picnic of chicken and peaches. In an instant, the Black Bear bounded along the beach, swam across the river and clambered up the other bank. Then only the sounds of it crashing through the underbrush convinced us it had really been there at all. For a long time we knelt in the river, wondering whether we were afraid of being devoured or offering ourselves to the jowls of the green woods.

An enormous weight— civilization, most likely — or the fear that nature was gone and we were in hell forever — fell away from me.

I had asked for some vision, some sign, some path: 'Artemis sent it,' I thought.

Every time I remember, I forget. We were walking down the trail, arguing. When I stopped and took off my glasses, I saw Actaeon with his splendid horns carefully pick his way behind a redwood stump and disappear. The last time I had seen him, he was slumping in the heavy sun of a Turkish zoo. I was so ashamed, I turned my back on him.

At sunset, we crossed the river away from the wild side. It was there the bear might come to drink. And the berries we were craving were also the bear's. Only those up the hill by the side of the road were ours.

On the fourth day, you put small, sometimes miniscule, stones in a circle. At the core, one rock embraced another. About them, in stone shawls and sombreros, saintly Madonnas and shepherds stood in majestic prayer. I brought a Tiki Poppa God stone to the outer circle, found a Momma stone, and a rocky embrace of mammals. In the third circle there was a single stone with a great force emanating from it, and alongside the labyrinth, a tree with a brain stone at the root, an owl, an eye of Horus, a pyramid, a little snake, an Aztec warrior, a sliver of crystal, whatever was needed to make a sacred world.

To protect the little world, we gathered logs and surrounded it in a triangle. At the apex we placed a uroborus of driftwood, fat stones suspended in its serpentine turns.

We were hiking toward the road when the sun was going down. Prayer at the end of the day. When we looked back toward our little world, we saw the giant of a man who'd been swimming downstream pitching the logs aside furiously, stamping on the sand in a mad jig, erasing every sign.

In the dream, after the radiation reached us, all the buildings would be left intact. We couldn't imagine the little world being destroyed. We had intended it as a gift to those who might come by. On the third day at the river, I had thought, 'This beauty comes from a great heart.'

"He doesn't know it's too late," I said. "The spirit has already entered the world through those stones. In his rampage, he is ravaging a pile of rubble."

On the last day of the river, we saw our monster foraging wildly in the blackberries by the road, oblivious to the thorns. The air was poisoned with his presence. Only when he left, were we brave enough to return to our spot on the river.

I had a great need to repair the little world. You said we could make another world, but it wasn't right. We couldn't discard that one as if it hadn't mattered at all.

We came to the site where the logs were thrown aside violently, like a pyramid of legs opened agape. It took a while to realize the little world was almost completely intact, that the litter was a sign that he'd stayed the night at this sacred spot, leaning up against the logs, watching a fire. Any careless movement of his leg would have tumbled the circle of stones.

We did a bit of repair as the day went on. When we left, I knelt down by the world and said:

"We did the best we could. We can't protect you more. As it is clear that barriers make enemies, you'll have to survive as is. Now you're on your own, go your way. You'll probably suffer like we do. Go out, as you must. You will forget. It is awful and inevitable. Then go down the hard path of mistaking everything before you remember."

On the last night, I dreamed the Camps. I called out, "Everyone who can escape, escape. Let the dog free. Take the gold and run." There was a guard now, and a gun, and a number and nothing I could do but offer up my life when the time came.

On the river, when I had come to see God with a great belly full of green and water, Her white egret spread its wings in the dark pool and flew languidly in a long dance down the full length of the river.

The faces of God in all the wild places which have not been touched by the hand. Eternity, they say, in the eye of the heart. Trees, hundreds of feet high, emerging for centuries out of their own fallen bodies. Be still. The bird brings the river from that highest mountain. Sit here your whole life, if you must, waiting for the blessing.

SONG

There are those who are trying to set fire to the world,
we are in danger,
there is time only to work slowly,
there is no time not to love.